ON THE MOUNTAIN

BY CHRISTOPHER SHINN

D1369768

DRAMATISTS
PLAY SERVICE
INC.

ON THE MOUNTAIN
Copyright © 2006, Christopher Shinn

All Rights Reserved

CAUTION: Professionals and amateurs are hereby warned that performance of ON THE MOUNTAIN is subject to payment of a royalty. It is fully protected under the copyright laws of the United States of America, and of all countries covered by the International Copyright Union (including the Dominion of Canada and the rest of the British Commonwealth), and of all countries covered by the Pan-American Copyright Convention, the Universal Copyright Convention, the Berne Convention, and of all countries with which the United States has reciprocal copyright relations. All rights, including professional/amateur stage rights, motion picture, recitation, lecturing, public reading, radio broadcasting, television, video or sound recording, all other forms of mechanical or electronic reproduction, such as CD-ROM, CD-I, DVD, information storage and retrieval systems and photocopying, and the rights of translation into foreign languages, are strictly reserved. Particular emphasis is placed upon the matter of readings, permission for which must be secured from the Author's agent in writing.

The English language stock and amateur stage performance rights in the United States, its territories, possessions and Canada for ON THE MOUNTAIN are controlled exclusively by DRAMATISTS PLAY SERVICE, INC., 440 Park Avenue South, New York, NY 10016. No professional or nonprofessional performance of the Play may be given without obtaining in advance the written permission of DRAMATISTS PLAY SERVICE, INC., and paying the requisite fee.

Inquiries concerning all other rights should be addressed to Creative Artists Agency, 162 Fifth Avenue, 6th Floor, New York, NY 10010. Attn: George Lane.

SPECIAL NOTE
Anyone receiving permission to produce ON THE MOUNTAIN is required to give credit to the Author as sole and exclusive Author of the Play on the title page of all programs distributed in connection with performances of the Play and in all instances in which the title of the Play appears for purposes of advertising, publicizing or otherwise exploiting the Play and/or a production thereof. The name of the Author must appear on a separate line, in which no other name appears, immediately beneath the title and in size of type equal to 50% of the size of the largest, most prominent letter used for the title of the Play. No person, firm or entity may receive credit larger or more prominent than that accorded the Author. The following acknowledgments must appear on the title page in all programs and on all posters distributed in connection with performances of the Play in size of type equal to not less than 35% of the size of the largest, most prominent letter used for the name of the Author:

Playwrights Horizons, Inc., New York City, produced the New York premiere of ON THE MOUNTAIN Off-Broadway in 2005.

Commissioned and first produced by South Coast Repertory.

ON THE MOUNTAIN was produced by South Coast Repertory, in Costa Mesa, California, opening on January 5, 2005. It was directed by Mark Rucker; the set design was by Donna Marquet; the costume design was by Melanie Watnick; the lighting design was by Rand Ryan; the original music and sound design were by Aram Arslanian; and the production manager was Jeff Gifford. The cast was as follows:

JAIME	Daisy Eagan
CARRICK	Nathan Baesel
SARAH	Susannah Schulman
PHIL	Matt Roth

ON THE MOUNTAIN was subsequently produced by Playwrights Horizons, in New York City, opening on February 4, 2005. It was directed by Jo Bonney; the set design was by Neil Patel; the costume design was by Mimi O'Donnell; the lighting design was by David Weiner; the sound design was by John Gromada; and the production stage manager was Judith Schoenfeld. The cast was as follows:

JAIME	Alison Pill
CARRICK	Ebon Moss-Bachrach
SARAH	Amy Ryan
PHIL	James Lloyd Reynolds

CHARACTERS

SARAH — 34. At once alert and tired. That she's largely given up on fashion and appearance in no way diminishes her considerable good looks. We can sense more than see that she was once beautiful. Measured, even wary, in her physicality, as though protecting herself from desire's destructive potential. Even so, her sexuality suffuses the most casual of gestures — she's hot despite herself.

JAIME — 16. Not pretty, although there is an innocence about her features that softens her some. But it must be said again: She is not pretty, and her mother knows this, as clearly as Jaime knows that her mother is good-looking. Overweight, moves awkwardly, as if unaware she has a body, her sexual yearning unintegrated with her physical being. Dresses in baggy clothes, doesn't wear makeup, has a pierced nose, etc.

CARRICK — 28. Lithe and winsome; works his charm a little too strenuously at times. A sense of inferiority hovers about him, but only a sensitive observer would note this. Has really nailed self-presentation — his clothes reveal his exquisite physique, and in a certain light he is shatteringly beautiful. Still, something is missing.

PHIL — Late 30s, in shape. Confident, somewhat high-strung, but undercuts his mania with humor and genuine feeling. Gets his clothes at the same places he shops for his teenage son.

PLACE

The setting is a small but well-kept home in Portland, Oregon. Front door leads to a sparsely decorated but cheery kitchen. From there we enter a small living room, made homey by a big, comfy sofa and cluttered coffee table. Against a wall is a computer desk and computer; above it hang framed some photographs, one large one of a little girl. A narrow stair leads up to bathroom and bedrooms, off. The back door opens onto a battered square of yard, where a few lawn chairs and some surrounding detritus live. A large tree looms unseen, throwing skeletal shadows down.

TIME

When the play begins it is summer 2003.

NOTE: A slash (/) in the text indicates when the next speaker or action begins. The play is written to be performed without an intermission.

I can scarcely bear my loss — I mean of the precious papers.

—Henry James, *The Aspern Papers*

ON THE MOUNTAIN

Scene 1

Night time. Quiet. Jaime is in the backyard, on a lawn chair, eyes shut, listening to an iPod, her head moving dreamily, a soda in her hand. Front door to house opens. Sarah enters, laughing, followed by Carrick.

SARAH. — the one I was *going* to was like a pick-up joint.

CARRICK. Really? But I thought, like, that's why people went to AA — to get laid.

SARAH. You've obviously never been to a meeting. Trust me:

CARRICK. — God, it's such a funny — *(Laughs.)*

SARAH. Trust me.

CARRICK. *(Exaggerated old man voice.)* "Back when I was a-drinkin' … had to walk three miles in the snow for a thimbleful o'moonshine!"

SARAH. I think *you* need to go to Smart Ass Anonymous.

CARRICK. Go? I wrote the book.

SARAH. Oh yeah?

CARRICK. Oh, Ashton Kutcher has nothing on me!

SARAH. *(Going into the kitchen.)* So what are the steps then?

CARRICK. The steps?

SARAH. The twelve steps.

CARRICK. Oh — the twelve steps. The twelve steps of Smart Ass Anonymous, let's see … Step one is pull my finger …

SARAH. *(Laughs.)* Uh-huh?

CARRICK. Step two is — oh, you spilled something on your shirt.

SARAH. *(Looking down.)* — I did? Where?

CARRICK. — Oh come on, you let me have that one.

SARAH. *(Laughs; as she gets herself a glass of water.)* Do you like

Ashton Kutcher?

CARRICK. Do I like Ashton Kutcher?

SARAH. What? I think he's cute.

CARRICK. Dude Where's My *Gun. (Sarah moves to the kitchen table with her water. Carrick looks around the living room. A moment.)*

SARAH. So, yeah, the meeting I go to — most of the guys are older, they've been sober twenty, thirty years some of them. Not just five minutes and all impressed with themselves. *(Carrick looks at a photograph of a girl, hanging on the wall above the computer.)*

CARRICK. I didn't picture your place like this.

SARAH. You had a mental picture of it?

CARRICK. Kind of.

SARAH. That's weird.

CARRICK. Why's that weird?

SARAH. Mental picture based on what?

CARRICK. I dunno — based on watching you at the restaurant ...

SARAH. *Watching* me? *(Carrick turns to Sarah.)*

CARRICK. Not, like, in a *pervy* way, just — like, the way you get a sense of someone by being around them.

SARAH. "A sense of someone" — I waited on you twice.

CARRICK. Tonight was the third time.

SARAH. Oh! So three times is the — the third time you got a mental picture of what my *house* looked like.

CARRICK. *(Coming over to table, sitting.)* Yeah! This isn't, like — I mean, *you* invited me over, right? *(Leaning in a little.)* So — you must have had a sense of me like I had a sense of you ...

SARAH. *(Beat.)* — All right, so, from "being around me" you thought my house looked like what?

CARRICK. *(Leaning back, laughing.)* Now I'm not gonna say!

SARAH. No, you have to — you said you didn't picture it like "this." What did you picture it like.

CARRICK. Well ... I pictured — I don't know, something kind of — dark and shadowy, like ... not a lot of stuff on the walls ...

SARAH. Dark and shadowy?

CARRICK. Yeah, like — I dunno. You're kind of mysterious.

SARAH. *(Laughs.)* I'm real mysterious. The mysterious waitress who works sixty hours a week!

CARRICK. No, I just mean, like — you don't talk about your past ...

SARAH. I've known you seven minutes.

CARRICK. Come on, we've talked at *least* an hour total, all added up.

SARAH. Yeah!

CARRICK. Hey, I need to know — it's the information age, total access, man.

SARAH. You can go on my website.

CARRICK. Really, you have a website? What's the address?

SARAH. W-w-w-dot-dark-and-mysterious-dot-com. *(Carrick laughs, which turns into a smile, which turns into a kiss. Carrick and Sarah kiss for a few moments, and then Sarah pulls away, smiling, and goes to the sink to refill her water.)* You want anything to drink?

CARRICK. *(As he takes out a pack of cigarettes.)* I'm okay. *(Carrick lights his cigarette. Sarah turns sharply.)*

SARAH. No smoking.

CARRICK. No? —

SARAH. Go out back. *(Sarah nods to the backyard.)*

CARRICK. Oh. *(Sarah turns, straightens up in the kitchen. Carrick goes out back. He fails to see Jaime — still listening to her iPod, eyes closed — as he takes out his cell phone and dials.)* Hey, what's up? Dude, you called me too much tonight. The store slow? No, but it's weird. No, I'm at her house — I know, right? No, I think she's into me. I don't know — she's actually kind of cool or whatever. No, she hasn't brought him up once, I tried to drop a few hints, like, about the kind of music I / like — *(Jaime smells the smoke and opens her eyes.)*

JAIME. Can I have one? *(Carrick jumps.)*

CARRICK. Jesus! *(Carrick shuts his cell phone, turns.)*

JAIME. *(Taking off her iPod.)* What?

CARRICK. I just said — Jesus — didn't see you.

JAIME. Oh, sorry. Listening to music. *(Carrick puts his phone away. Jaime finishes her soda.)*

CARRICK. You wanted a smoke?

JAIME. Yeah, if that's cool. *(Carrick takes a cigarette out of his pack. Jaime gets up, takes it.)*

CARRICK. Are you — you live here?

JAIME. Yup. Sarah's my mom.

CARRICK. Your — mom?

JAIME. *(Laughs.)* Guess she didn't tell you yet!

CARRICK. No, we just — wow. *(Carrick reaches to light Jaime's cigarette, just as she pulls out her own lighter. As she moves back to the chair:)*

JAIME. Usually she tells people, she blabs about me all the time,

11

it drives me crazy.

CARRICK. So are you the — in the picture, the little / girl —

JAIME. Ugh, I hate that picture! For some reason it's like her favorite picture of me or whatever. I hate it! — Also she doesn't let me smoke inside the house. Which is like, it totally interrupts my rhythm when I'm writing. Plus she smells like smoke anyway, from the restaurant, so I'm like, What's the big deal, let me smoke in the house. Not to mention there are pictures of her literally *breast*feeding me with a cigarette in her mouth.

CARRICK. For real?

JAIME. *(Exhaling.)* What are these?

CARRICK. Reds?

JAIME. — Oh my God, total déjà vu. I was at the mall this one time with my friend Deena — wait, what's your name?

CARRICK. I'm Carrick.

JAIME. Carrick? I like that, it's poetic. Your parents had a sense of style.

CARRICK. Um — I found the name on the Internet actually. They named me something else.

JAIME. What?

CARRICK. Honestly? I don't really even tell people anymore.

JAIME. You don't get along with them?

CARRICK. Could say that.

JAIME. Yeah, my mom doesn't talk to her folks, either. *(Jaime makes a "drinking" motion. Carrick nods.)* That's cool that you gave yourself your own name, though. I'm Jaime, j-a-*i*-m-e. It means "I love" in French if you spell it that way — but, so my friend Deena — we were in the mall, and this guy, this weird, like, short eighteen-year-old guy with a big bushy beard came over to us and asked us if we wanted a cigarette. We were twelve, we had never had a cigarette before, so we went out with him, and he gave us each a red. And then he talked for like fifteen minutes about Phish — the band Phish, not the fish fish. *(Sarah begins to cross from the kitchen to the backyard.)*

CARRICK. Phish — there's a blast from the past.

JAIME. Were you into Phish?

CARRICK. I wasn't really, but these guys I used to smoke pot with were.

JAIME. Yeah, I guess they're okay if you're stoned. *(Carrick laughs, Sarah opens the door, sees Jaime.)* Hi. Smoker's exile. *(Carrick turns, sees Sarah. Pause.)*

SARAH. You're up.

JAIME. I started a new story.

SARAH. A new one? What's it about.

JAIME. *Mom.*

SARAH. *(Smiles.)* Stinks out here. *(Sarah goes back into the house.)*

JAIME. She always wants to know what they're "about." *(Carrick smiles.)*

CARRICK. Should probably ... *(Nods towards house.)*

JAIME. Sure. *(Carrick puts out cigarette, starts inside. Jaime follows him.)* I've been listening to Radiohead all night, I feel like I'm going out of my mind.

CARRICK. Yeah, Radiohead'll do it to you.

JAIME. Do you like them?

CARRICK. Um — yes and no? I'm not really hip to the whole hyper-produced weird electronic dystopia thing. *(They enter kitchen, where Sarah is.)*

JAIME. Who do you listen to?

CARRICK. Honestly, I work at Sam Goody, and I have this really wack manager named Jack who's always playing totally crap Top 40 all day, so I kind of got turned off to anything new. I'm more, like, into early 90s stuff — Smashing Pumpkins, Pixies, Pavement, Tori Amos ...

JAIME. Oh my God, I love Tori Amos, you listen to Tori Amos?

CARRICK. Oh, totally.

JAIME. I never met a guy who liked her, most guys are like — who else do you listen to?

CARRICK. Um ... I like Radiohead's first couple of albums ... And Ration, Ration was probably my — Jason Carlyle just — the most real, like — he was singing my life for me, you know? *(Pause. Jaime looks at Sarah.)*

SARAH. Jaime tries to get me to listen to Radiohead, but I can never understand their lyrics.

CARRICK. Yeah — it's like Thom Yorke has a moral objection to enunciation.

SARAH. That, but also what they mean. What do they mean? Nothing.

JAIME. They're not supposed to "mean" — *(to Carrick.)* this is like a constant conversation. She thinks lyrics have to say exactly what they mean.

SARAH. Jaime has a thing now about not making sense. She / has this —

JAIME. Here we go —

SARAH. — this, teacher who, who told her that / her

JAIME. Oh my God!

SARAH. Stories don't need to make sense. That her stories don't actually have to *tell* a story.

JAIME. That's not what Elaine says, she doesn't say stories don't have to tell / a story —

SARAH. She said, what did she say to you? "Your stories aren't confusing enough."

JAIME. What she meant was — first of all, you can call her a therapist, I'm not, like, ashamed. *(To Carrick.)* She runs this group I go to, her name is Elaine. She said that my stories made too *much* sense, not that they shouldn't make *any* sense.

SARAH. So now she's writing stories that — I have stories from when she was thirteen and fourteen that were these / great —

JAIME. They are the worst stories!

SARAH. They are not!

JAIME. *(To Carrick.)* Elaine is trying to get me to write more out of my unconscious.

SARAH. I still don't understand what that / means. *(Cell phone rings. Jaime checks it.)*

JAIME. Deena.

SARAH. She's calling late.

JAIME. I went over her house tonight? So listen to what happened. We were about to have ice cream, we open the pint of Ben and Jerry's, me and Deena and Chris, and / we're —

SARAH. Wait, who's Chris?

JAIME. Just this guy.

SARAH. From school?

JAIME. He's a mechanic, Deena / just

SARAH. A mechanic?

JAIME. Deena just met him or whatever, they're friends. He's not — he's kind of a geek, he's all into these night vision goggles he has, supposedly he drives around at night and watches people have sex in cars and in parks and stuff.

CARRICK. Whoa.

SARAH. How old is he?

JAIME. Anyway, so Deena's dad comes home — he got fired from his job, again, and he's drunk, of course, and he's like, What are you doing, and we're like, Having some ice cream. So he grabs the pint, just takes it — and starts licking it. Like licks the whole top of the ice cream, not just once, but like *keeps* licking it over and over.

SARAH. How many jobs has he lost now? What are they gonna do?

JAIME. He told Deena it's okay that he got fired, because he just got some job building a new golf course in Arizona for a month. So he's gonna leave Deena alone while he / does the job. *(Jaime's phone rings again; she looks at it, turns, goes, answering:)* Hey — What's up? What? Oh my God! *(She goes upstairs, off. Pause. Carrick looks at Sarah.)*

SARAH. I know.

CARRICK. What?

SARAH. Like what planet did she come from.

CARRICK. No — she seems really cool. *(Nodding to the computer area.)* I was wondering who the picture was.

SARAH. Yeah. She's three years old there … I didn't mean "what planet" in a bad way. I just meant … She's sixteen but she's more like — she wants to be a writer, she reads all the time, she's kinda …

CARRICK. She seems like a normal kid — into her iPod, her cell phone …

SARAH. Yeah, she's not into the bills, though. That cell phone bill is out of / control —

CARRICK. Is her dad around? *(Pause. Sarah sits down at the kitchen table.)*

SARAH. — Probably in some junkie hotel somewhere, who knows.

CARRICK. Seriously?

SARAH. He was just this one night thing. Met him at a party, he was in a band. He had a mohawk, played me his demo … Never saw him again.

CARRICK. *(Moving to table.)* How old were you when you had her?

SARAH. Eighteen.

CARRICK. Wow. And you decided to …

SARAH. God, we're getting heavy!

CARRICK. Sorry — I didn't mean to — So Jaime likes Radiohead, you're not really into them, that's cool. What do you listen to? *(Sarah smiles. Pause.)*

SARAH. Whatever's on the radio.

CARRICK. Come on.

SARAH. I used to be into the, the whole music scene, I'm not really — I don't follow things anymore, I work so much, I don't have time. Just turn on the radio, whatever's playing … *(Pause.)* She changed my life. Saved it.

CARRICK. You don't have any help? *(Sarah shakes her head "no."*

Pause. Then:)

SARAH. Couple months ago I had to take her out of school — that's been a trip.

CARRICK. She doesn't go to school?

SARAH. She has depression. One day, she just — wouldn't go to school, wouldn't get out of bed — took her to a shrink, he put her on Prozac … They say it's a disease, you can't control it, just hope, you know, that you keep treating it and — the shrink said hopefully she'll feel better by the fall and then she'll go back — *(Jaime bounds down the stairs. Carrick and Sarah turn.)*

JAIME. Deena's dad got arrested.

SARAH. For what?

JAIME. I guess after I left he went out to a bar and smashed a bottle of beer against a pinball machine, and he cut his hand. So he got arrested, and he ended up getting like twenty stitches — and that job was supposed to start in two days, so now he can't do it.

SARAH. There you go.

JAIME. So … *(Jaime looks at Carrick, then her mother. She smiles.)* Okay, I'm gonna play some music and go to bed.

SARAH. Good night.

CARRICK. Night. *(She runs back up the stairs and off. Pause. Carrick looks at Sarah, smiles. He leans in to kiss her. As they kiss, a blast of music sounds from upstairs.)*

Scene 2

A few weeks later. Jaime sits at the computer, typing. Her iPod is plugged into the computer. Music plays loudly through the speakers. She swigs from a can of soda. Front door opens. Carrick peeks in. Calls out:

CARRICK. Jaime? *(She doesn't respond. He steps into the house, carrying a bouquet of roses.)* Jaime. *(Still no response. He approaches Jaime. Jaime turns, startled.)* Sorry —

JAIME. Hey — *(Jaime turns, closes her file.)*

CARRICK. I knocked, but no one was / answering *(Jaime turns off the iPod, the music stops.)* the door. So …

16

JAIME. I was just —

CARRICK. Writing.

JAIME. Yeah. My mom's in the shower I think.

CARRICK. *(Putting roses down on table.)* Cool, yeah, I just wanted to stop by before she went to AA. I'll wait out back, if you could tell her I'm ... *(Carrick starts to go out back.)*

JAIME. — Can I bum a red?

CARRICK. *(Stops, turns, smiles.)* Sure.

JAIME. Thanks. *(She follows him outside.)* I'm doing one of my iPod afternoons, putting all these new songs on it.

CARRICK. Yeah?

JAIME. I have like over eight hundred songs on it now, it's like — there's literally no mood you're in where you don't have a song that matches it. *(Carrick hands her a cigarette.)*

CARRICK. Your own private soundtrack to your life.

JAIME. Yeah. *(Carrick lights his cigarette, looks up at the sky.)* Did my mom tell you about Deena?

CARRICK. No, did something happen?

JAIME. Her dad has this pocketknife that he's had for a really long time, I guess, and Chris was playing with it while we were watching TV the other night? So her dad comes home, drunk, sees him playing with it, *totally* flips out, goes crazy yelling, and tries to grab it — but because he's so drunk he ends up missing, and he sort of like *pokes* Chris in the eye? So then Chris gets all mad and he swings back, and Deena's dad tries to block him? Chris ends up *hitting* his hand — the one with the cut.

CARRICK. Ow!

JAIME. Wicked hard, totally opens it up again, two weeks after he got all the stitches.

CARRICK. That is brutal.

JAIME. Yeah, but now he's scamming his doctor for more Vicodin — Can I have a light?

CARRICK. Oh — sure ...

JAIME. *(Shaking her lighter, smiles.)* Ran out of fluid. *(Carrick holds out his lighter, Jaime leans in. She drags, exhales, smiles, looks off. Pause.)*

CARRICK. Hey, so — I don't know what you — heard last night, but ... if you did, you know, I just — want to apologize for that. I'm sorry.

JAIME. I didn't hear anything ...

CARRICK. — Just in case you did or whatever. So ... *(Pause.)* What are you writing?

JAIME. Still the story, still working on it.

CARRICK. Same one you won't talk about?

JAIME. Yeah … still trying to figure out what it's about, like … *(Pause.)* — You can read it if you want.

CARRICK. Really?

JAIME. If you / want — *(Sarah opens the back door. Carrick turns. Pause.)*

CARRICK. Hey. *(Pause. Sarah stares blankly at him.)* Just getting the gossip …

JAIME. — About Deena's dad.

SARAH. Uh-huh? *(Pause.)*

CARRICK. Was in the 'hood …

SARAH. I have to go to my meeting.

CARRICK. Right on. *(Sarah goes into the house. Carrick puts out his cigarette and follows her into the kitchen. Jaime stays outside, smoking. She moves close to the door and inconspicuously listens.)* I — brought some roses for / you —

SARAH. I see, thanks. *(Pause.)*

CARRICK. I've been thinking about why I freaked out last night and — I wanted to say I'm sorry. I shouldn't have. *(Pause.)*

SARAH. I can't get into a whole conversation, my meeting starts / at seven —

CARRICK. I really like hanging out with you. *(Pause.)* I know it hasn't been that long, but —

SARAH. Exactly, which is why you asking me why I haven't, why I'm not, or, accusing / me of —

CARRICK. Sarah, if you don't want to share your past then — that's your right, I have no / right —

SARAH. It's not about "sharing" or — it's you getting paranoid and freaking out / like I'm —

CARRICK. Are you free tomorrow night? *(Sarah smiles.)* I wanna make it up to you, let me take you out.

SARAH. I'm working all day, I have a lot of errands to do after work.

CARRICK. Right … *(Pause. Sarah goes to her purse, goes through it. Carrick turns away. Jaime enters, goes to the computer, types. Carrick brings the roses from the table to the counter. Conversationally:)* So I'll be at Goody later, if you wanna come by. I got this kind of weird call — this girl Donna got fired, she's a really good employee, and she called me crying, she said Jack just flipped out on her, she has no idea why. So I told her I'd go ask Jack what happened. *(Sarah looks up from her purse.)* So — if you wanna stop by, or …

SARAH. It's gonna be an early night for me.

CARRICK. Right … you know, just in case — Bye. *(Carrick starts to go.)*

JAIME. — Wait. *(Carrick turns.)* I have the story.

CARRICK. Oh, cool. *(Jaime takes the story from the printer, goes to Carrick, hands it to him.)* "Elizabeth's Necklace."

JAIME. If you don't get it — it's totally fine. I'm still working on it.

CARRICK. I can't wait to read it. *(Jaime smiles. Pause. Carrick looks at Sarah, smiles, exits, off. Sarah gathers her things.)*

JAIME. You're going to AA?

SARAH. You know that's where I'm going.

JAIME. Jesus. Just making conversation. *(Jaime goes back to the computer, sits. We hear Carrick's car pull away. Sarah is about to exit when music comes on, loud, over the speakers. Sarah stops, turns. Jaime has her iPod in her hand.)*

SARAH. Jaime.

JAIME. *(Turns, lowers volume on music.)* What?

SARAH. Did he say something to you?

JAIME. What?

SARAH. Carrick, did he ask you about anything?

JAIME. About … what?

SARAH. Why did you put that on just now?

JAIME. I don't know, just felt like it.

SARAH. Carrick didn't say anything?

JAIME. About Ration?

SARAH. Yeah.

JAIME. No, why? *(Pause.)*

SARAH. You never said anything, he never asked you / anything?

JAIME. No, why are you being all weird? *(Pause.)*

SARAH. He knows about Jason. *(Pause. Jaime turns off the music. Sarah sits at the kitchen table.)* Last night, we were watching a movie, everything was fine, then out of nowhere he said, "Did you know Jason Carlyle?" And I said no —

JAIME. You said no?

SARAH. I just — I just blanked, I didn't …

JAIME. How did he hear?

SARAH. He said — he typed my name into the Internet or something, just randomly, and some thing came up that said that I knew him.

JAIME. What site?

SARAH. I don't know, he didn't say. *(Jaime turns, starts typing on the computer.)* So I was like, Okay, you got me, I did know him. And he was all upset that I hadn't told him, and that I had "lied." You didn't hear us fighting?

JAIME. No, I just — I heard, like, yelling, but ... so, what happened?

SARAH. He was all like, why hadn't I told him, then why did I lie / when he asked —

JAIME. What did you end up telling him?

SARAH. I tried to say, it's not a — I don't think about him, I told him that — it wasn't a big deal, that I knew him in high school, that we knew each other a little — You know what, I don't have — *(Starts to gather things.)* I don't have time ... *(Sarah begins to go. Jaime types on Internet rapidly.)*

JAIME. It *is* online.

SARAH. *(Stopping.)* What?

JAIME. "Sarah Scott was part of the Seattle scene."

SARAH. — It says that?

JAIME. "She and Jason dated before Ration got big."

SARAH. *(Moving to the computer.)* Who wrote this?

JAIME. "Despite his marriage to Lobe lead singer Kelly Hatch, Jason kept a flame alive for Sarah, and it's rumored that he left her a CD containing his final song."

SARAH. That's ridiculous.

JAIME. "Kelly Hatch was on tour when Jason's body was discovered. Police photos of his body taken as a part of the investigation into the supposed suicide / show ... "

SARAH. I can't believe this, unbelievable —

JAIME. "Sarah moved to Portland following Jason's death in 1994." Is that you? *(Sarah moves closer, looks at the computer.)*

SARAH. Oh my God.

JAIME. You look hot!

SARAH. I can't even — do you know how wasted I am in that picture? *(Sarah turns away, goes to her pocketbook. Jaime turns to her.)*

JAIME. So — what happened with Carrick?

SARAH. He kept saying I was lying to him, I said, No I'm not.

JAIME. But — you were.

SARAH. *(Stopping.)* No I wasn't.

JAIME. You told him you didn't know Jason.

SARAH. It's none of his business! But then I told him I *did* know him.

JAIME. That's it?

SARAH. Jaime, I don't, I don't go around telling everybody everything, that's not my / style.

JAIME. You guys were in love. You and Jason loved each / other.

SARAH. That was — what difference does it make to Carrick if, we were in love?

JAIME. He likes you — he wants to know you.

SARAH. — I don't like talking about that time, that was a really destructive time in my life.

JAIME. So fine, so tell him it was a bad time — he just wants to know you.

SARAH. Well, he should want to know me now, not who I was then.

JAIME. But — who you were then, like — is why you are who you are now. *(Pause.)*

SARAH. I'm late for my meeting. *(Sarah goes, off.)*

Scene 3

Later that night. Door opens. Sarah enters, followed by Carrick.

CARRICK. — I mean, How can you have a manager who is — and Jack's in charge of hiring at the store, he's in charge of everything / basically. *(Sarah sees the roses, arranged in a vase on the kitchen table.)*

SARAH. Look — Jaime put the roses … *(Carrick looks at them and smiles. Sarah reads from a piece of paper next to the vase.)* "Mom, went to Deena's, be back later. I love you." Awww.

CARRICK. — Then it's like, if Jack's in charge of everything, how do you even start / to — *(Sarah crosses into kitchen. Carrick sits down at the kitchen table. As he speaks, Sarah puts away some groceries and dishes up two small bowls of ice cream.)*

SARAH. How did you find all this out?

CARRICK. By the time I got there Jack had left, so I talked to one of the CSRs — and she / told me —

SARAH. CS? …

CARRICK. R. Customer Service Representative — cashier, basically

— and she told me, she filled me in, said Jack had been stealing for *months*. And a lot of people have known but they're keeping quiet, 'cuz what are they supposed to do? He's the boss.

SARAH. How is he stealing from the store, aren't there safeguards...?

CARRICK. It's really clever — he'll say, Oh, the store needs a vacuum, and he'll use his own money to buy a vacuum cleaner, hand the receipt into the regional office and get reimbursed. But he'll have a copy of the receipt and then he'll return the vacuum cleaner to the store he bought it from and get his own money back too. He's been doing this with everything you can imagine, so, like, he bought all these Christmas decorations, which is not something Sam Goody corporate already does —

SARAH. But why doesn't someone just tell the regional office?

CARRICK. 'Cuz Jack is really tight with the regional manager, so everyone's scared of getting laid off. I don't know, maybe since she got fired Donna will say something. Supposedly the guy Jack hired to replace Donna is, like, a drug buddy of his, shows up for work an hour late, totally tweaking. *(Sarah brings over two bowls of ice cream, and the pint.)*

SARAH. See — I bet this is going to take care of itself.

CARRICK. What do you mean?

SARAH. This is what's gonna happen, I've heard this story a million times: Jack will keep pressing his luck, till the regional office puts two and two together. Or he'll hit bottom and go way overboard and break into the store and rob it — that kind of thing. The addiction always takes over, it controls you, you don't control it.

CARRICK. God. I feel bad for the guy — he's a dick, but, like, he could go to jail for this. *(Carrick picks up his spoon. Sarah goes into the living room, to the computer desk. She takes a photo album off it and opens it.)* Also, it's like — how did I miss this? How did I not know what was going on?

SARAH. It's amazing how you can cover. I was working two jobs plus raising Jaime when I was drinking — and no one knew, no one at work, no one at Jaime's school ... I'd have friends over, they'd leave, four in the morning, I'd be up at seven to drive Jaime to school. *(Sarah flips through the photo album. Carrick looks down at his ice cream.)*

CARRICK. Step one: We admitted we were powerless over Ben and Jerry's Cherry Garcia. *(Carrick takes a bite of ice cream. Sarah continues to look at the photo album. Carrick looks at her. Pause.)* You're melting ... *(Sarah continues to look at the album. After a moment, she comes to the kitchen table, holding open the album. She puts it down in front of Carrick.)* Oh — my God!

SARAH. I don't have that many pictures of him. Which is funny because there must be a million pictures of him but ... I really knew him before he got famous, so — if I'd known, I would have taken more pictures. *(Carrick puts down his spoon, looks at the album.)* I'm sorry for not telling you. *(Carrick looks up at her.)* I don't even talk about it in AA. When I moved here it was like — I was just so happy to go somewhere where no one knew me, knew that part of my life, I just — put it away. *(Pause. Sarah moves her chair over, closer to Carrick's, and sits. They look together at the pictures. As they do, Carrick reaches for Sarah's hand and holds it. Carrick laughs, intensely looking.)* What.

CARRICK. So you guys ...

SARAH. ... Yeah, we were pretty serious about each other — God. I'm fucked up in every picture here.

CARRICK. — Jesus, Sarah! Look at how he's looking at you!

SARAH. I — know it happened, I know I had the feelings but — when you get sober, it's like — the old life — it feels like it happened to someone else. Not you. And in a way it wasn't you, it wasn't the real you.

CARRICK. — Is that Jaime? Ha!

SARAH. *(Smiling.)* Yeah. That's — the picture of Jaime on the wall is from the same day. Jason took them. Jaime was getting older and I decided to stop drinking for the hundredth time, and Jason was trying to stop using like he always was, so we had this idea that we would have this picnic to start us off on our new sober life ... We made sandwiches, he brought his camera.

CARRICK. He looks so — it's not like the other pictures — he looks — almost fragile, like, delicate ...

SARAH. Every time he was with Jaime he just — it was like he got lighter, his eyes, something just — lifted ...

CARRICK. So — *Jason's* Jaime's dad.

SARAH. No — we weren't even talking when I got pregnant. One day, I don't remember what happened exactly, but I'd had a bad day, and I told some friend, this friend we both knew, that I was gonna get an abortion. Couple hours later, out of nowhere, knock on my door — Jason. Comes in, puts his cheek on my stomach, starts singing this lullaby ... says, "This baby's gonna be the best thing that ever happened to us. The best thing." *(Pause.)* — He loved her, he played with her all the time, for hours — look at her here.

CARRICK. Like *she's* in love. *(Flipping through more pictures.)* — Wow. Unfuckingbelievable …

SARAH. I think it was — a couple weeks after this, after the picnic, he called me up crying. "It finally happened, it finally happened."

CARRICK. What?

SARAH. "We got a deal, we got signed, we're having a party, get over here."

CARRICK. Yeah!

SARAH. Some rich dude's house, I left Jaime with a friend … I remember getting there and — I mean, there were always other girls, you know, and hangers-on and all that, but this was this *whole* other — the girls, I'd never seen these girls before, and there were guys in suits all over the place and just — *all* these *people* — finally I find Jason, he says he's sorry it's so crazy, tells me to go upstairs, there's a room at the end of the hallway and he'll come up in a couple of minutes. So I grab a bottle, go up …

CARRICK. You were still drinking.

SARAH. Oh yeah, the picnic — no. No, I didn't get sober till he died. So I'm up there — hour. Wait. Two hours … Now I'm wasted, I start looking around, opening doors — house is huge. Finally I find him — in some little room, in the dark, him and a couple of random guys, nodding off. He looks at me … And I just … *(Pause.)* The picnic's my last real memory of him. I mean, he called me a couple of times when he was touring, but — basically he got famous, he met Kelly, and that was that. *(Pause. Sarah picks up the pint of ice cream, brings it to the freezer. She comes back to the table, takes her bowl, brings it to the sink.)*

CARRICK. You're not gonna eat your ice cream?

SARAH. I'm not really hungry. *(Sarah begins washing her bowl. Pause. Carrick picks up his bowl, brings it over.)* You can eat yours.

CARRICK. No, I'm okay.

SARAH. Don't be silly, eat it.

CARRICK. I'm done. *(Pause. Sarah takes his bowl, puts it in the sink, starts to wash it. Carrick watches her. She looks over at him and laughs — he looks away. She turns back to the dishes. Pause. Brightly:)* I read Jaime's story!

SARAH. Oh yeah?

CARRICK. Yeah, at Goody — I went out to have a smoke, thought I'd just look at the first page — I couldn't stop.

SARAH. — So it's good?

CARRICK. Oh, Sarah, it's amazing. I should leave her a note, tell her how much I liked it. *(Carrick sits down at the kitchen table, begins to write on the reverse of the note Jaime left for Sarah.)*

SARAH. It's not a "doesn't make any sense" story?

CARRICK. *(Writing.)* No, it makes total sense. *(Reading what he wrote.)* "Jaime, your story rocks." That sounded better in my head. *(Keeps writing.)*

SARAH. I really think she could be a professional, I mean. We'd work so hard, when she was a little girl, you know, I'd help her with her stories, for *hours,* I saw how talented she was. That's why I get so worried with Elaine telling her all this weird stuff about not making sense and the unconscious and all that. Jaime won't show me anymore, I don't even know what she's writing.

CARRICK. *(Stops writing, puts down pen.)* This one — It's about this girl, Lucy, who has these two friends, Elizabeth and Tim, and they're all like thirteen. They're at Lucy's house, they're in the backyard, late at night, stoned, hanging out — and Lucy ends up dozing, right?

SARAH. *(Still doing dishes.)* Uh-huh?

CARRICK. So Elizabeth and Tim decide — they come up with this idea to make a huge bowl of cereal to eat — So they go inside, get this huge, like, mixing bowl, and they pour all these cereals in — everything, Cocoa Puffs, Cheerios, Raisin Bran, Life — nasty! And they pour all this milk in, right, and get these big spoons and sit down and start munching, and immediately they're like, it's gross, they can't eat it. Then Elizabeth looks into the living room and she starts, like, giggling, and Tim is like, What? Tim looks — it's Lucy's dad. Passed out in front of the TV, wearing just his boxers — and they're really old boxers and he's sort of hanging out of them a little, his dick and balls.

SARAH. *(Turning.)* What?

CARRICK. No, it's good!

SARAH. *(Turns off faucet.)* See, she would never put something like that in before Elaine.

CARRICK. But listen: *(As Carrick speaks, he gets up, he moves around, remembering the story, moving into the living room. Sarah listens as she wipes down the kitchen table.)* So Elizabeth knows that Lucy has this Polaroid in her room, and she gets this idea. She dares Tim to take a picture of Lucy's dad in his underwear. Tim's like, No way, so Elizabeth says that if *he* takes a picture of Lucy's dad, she'll let him take pictures of *her* with her *shirt* off. So Tim's like, Okay — they get the Polaroid, sneak into the living room, take the picture — then the two of them run into the bathroom, lock the door and wait. They're shaking the picture, waiting for it to fill in — it turns out, it's a perfect shot. So Elizabeth's like — Okay. And she takes off her shirt. Tim starts taking pictures, he takes like four pictures when — knock on the bathroom door. *(Sarah looks up.)* It's Lucy, and Lucy's like, Open up. Tim, like, panics, stuffs all the pictures in his pocket, and Elizabeth hides the Polaroid in the hamper, puts on her shirt, and they open the door — and just kind of walk out like nothing's weird, like, Hey. *(Sarah finishes wiping the table. She sits down, closes the photo album, and watches Carrick.)* So. Lucy goes in to pee. She's peeing, when she sees something — it's one of the pictures, it fell out of Tim's pocket. It's just sort of this blur — this pinkish blur. But then Lucy sees — she recognizes Elizabeth's necklace. She sees that it's a picture of Elizabeth's neck.

She goes into the kitchen. Elizabeth and Tim are pouring the big bowl of cereal into the sink, and they're laughing. Lucy looks at the Polaroid and she starts to feel like she's going to cry — but then, like, something comes over her. And she puts the picture in her pocket and goes over to the sink. Elizabeth and Tim are playing with the cereal, mushing it around with their fingers, like. And Lucy watches them for a second ... and then *she* starts laughing too. And puts *her* hands in the cereal. And they all just do this, all three of them keep playing with the cereal and laughing — except every once in a while, Lucy looks over at Elizabeth's necklace — just stares at it, the little glass pendant dangling. And that's the end. *(Carrick smiles. Pause.)*

SARAH. I don't — think I get it.

CARRICK. Really?

SARAH. I don't get the ending, why does she start laughing?

CARRICK. Oh, that's the best — because, like ... *(Pause.)* I mean, you could interpret it different ways, but — for me ... Okay: the last girl I loved? Her name was Doris. And she was in a band. We went out for three years — we lived together. The night she broke up with me, she told me she was in love with Kevin — the bassist. And — then she told me they'd been sleeping together for a year. *(Carrick looks away, laughs.)* I never told anyone that last part. *(Carrick looks back to Sarah.)* And do you know what I did? After she told me that? I kept going to their gigs! Hanging out with them, partying with them — playing their music in my car when I drove to work in the morning. You know? That thing of like — something happens, and it's *so* not what you wanted that — you can't even *feel* it — 'cuz if you feel it you're gonna ... like ... *(Pause.*

26

Carrick laughs, wipes away a tear. Sarah gets up from the table. She moves awkwardly past Carrick and goes to the photograph of Jaime hanging on the wall. Carrick watches as she takes down the picture and undoes the back of the frame. She removes a CD from it.) Oh my … *(Sarah turns to Carrick, holding the CD. Pause.)*

SARAH. No one knows about it. Not even Jaime.

CARRICK. Holy …

SARAH. He wrote it when we were in high school … He took this poem from my journal and made it into a song. He said he'd never record it, he wanted it to be just for us. They found it — when he died. It's just him and a guitar. No one's ever heard it except me. *(Pause.)* Come upstairs, we'll play it in my bedroom. *(Sarah starts towards the stairs.)*

CARRICK. Wait. *(Sarah stops.)* There's something I need to tell you.

SARAH. What?

CARRICK. When you came into the store — when I saw your name on the credit card … I recognized it. From that website. That's — why I started talking to you and why I started hanging out at the restaurant.

SARAH. You — knew me from / the —

CARRICK. I thought — I don't know, I just thought maybe I could, like, hang out with you and maybe hear — if there really was a song, hear it. I didn't — these last couple weeks … *(Pause. Sarah looks away.)* I didn't know I was gonna start falling in love with you. *(Pause. Sarah looks back at him.)* Put it back.

SARAH. What.

CARRICK. The CD. Put it back. *(Pause. Sarah replaces the CD in the back of the frame. Carrick moves in to her, kisses her.)*

SARAH. Oh God — Carrick — *(She puts the photograph down on the desk. They continue to kiss, quickly escalating. Then Sarah takes Carrick's hand, looks at him, and leads him by the hand up the stairs and off. Front door opens. Jaime enters, wearing her iPod. She goes to the fridge, takes out a slice of pizza and a soda. She sees the photo album on the kitchen table, flips through it. She looks at the unfinished note from Carrick beside it. She takes off her iPod, listens for sounds of wakefulness — the house is silent. Jaime moves to the computer, sits, puts down her soda. Takes a bite of pizza, sees the photograph of her sitting on the desk. She puts down the slice, picks up the photograph. The back comes off and the CD falls out. Jaime bends down and picks up the CD. From upstairs come sounds of lovemaking. Jaime looks at the CD, then up towards the sounds.)*

27

Scene 4

Later that week. Early afternoon. Sarah is in the kitchen, making sandwiches and putting them into a cooler. Front door opens. Jaime enters, goes to refrigerator.

SARAH. You're back. What took you so long?

JAIME. *(Opening refrigerator.)* The group went late.

SARAH. We're leaving in / a —

JAIME. Where's the soda?

SARAH. I packed it for Mount Rainier. Carrick's getting dressed, we have to leave, are you all ready?

JAIME. *(Goes to cooler, takes out a soda.)* I don't think I'm gonna go. *(Pause.)*

SARAH. Why not?

JAIME. I just don't feel like it.

SARAH. Is something going on tonight?

JAIME. *(Putting soda in refrigerator.)* No. *(Jaime goes out back. She lights a cigarette and puts on her iPod. Carrick hustles down the stairs, hair wet from shower.)*

CARRICK. We gotta go, we gotta go, let's move it! Jaime back?

SARAH. Yeah — she says she's not coming.

CARRICK. *(Stops.)* What?

SARAH. I know. She's still in this mood. I don't know what it is.

CARRICK. The group didn't help?

SARAH. I guess not.

CARRICK. What did she say?

SARAH. She doesn't wanna go, she doesn't feel like it.

CARRICK. Let me see what's up.

SARAH. Good luck. *(Carrick goes out back and finds Jaime smoking.)*

CARRICK. *(Fake British accent.)* Bum a fag? *(Jaime turns, looks at Carrick as if she heard but didn't understand. Carrick makes a "smoking" motion. Jaime takes out a cigarette. Hands it to him. He then motions for her to take off the iPod. She takes the earphones off.)* How did your group go?

JAIME. Okay.

CARRICK. Yeah? Anything going on, any new dramas?

JAIME. Not really. Toby finally came out to his parents, he talked about that …

CARRICK. Yeah?

JAIME. Yeah … but he chickened out at the last minute and told them he was bi? It turns out that they already *thought* he was gay, so when he told them he was bi, they were all like relieved and jumping for joy.

CARRICK. Oh no!

JAIME. Yeah … *(Pause. Jaime looks off.)*

CARRICK. So — your mom says you're bailing on Mount Rainier?

JAIME. *(Laughs.)* Not "bailing," but …

CARRICK. Probably nice to have the whole house to yourself — chill out, write …

JAIME. Yeah … I'm — I don't know.

CARRICK. What? *(Pause.)*

JAIME. Nothing, just — it's like I'm having trouble writing lately.

CARRICK. Really?

JAIME. I *want* to write … it's weird. *(Pause.)*

CARRICK. Is something going on, or? …

JAIME. … No. I mean … *(Pause.)* I don't know. Like — Deena started going out with Chris? And, I don't know, it's fine, I just … — I don't know, whatever. *(Jaime laughs, looks away. Pause.)*

CARRICK. Well, I know you said you'd rather hang out here this weekend, but — I was really looking forward to you coming with us.

JAIME. Oh …

CARRICK. Have you ever been? *(Jaime shakes her head "no.")* I know camping can sound, like, a bit nerdy, but — when you get up there it's like — on the mountain — the sky — looking up at the stars — Jaime, it's like — seeing God … or Goddess, or, or whatever you believe / in —

JAIME. *(Laughing.)* "A Power greater than ourselves."

CARRICK. *(Laughs.)* Right! Exactly! *(Pause.)*

JAIME. How long … Are you guys, how long is the trip gonna …?

CARRICK. Just the night, come back tomorrow. *(Jaime nods. Pause. Carrick looks up at the sky.)* Perfect / weather —

JAIME. Yeah, I'll go — *(Carrick looks back to Jaime. Pause.)*

CARRICK. What?

JAIME. What?

CARRICK. No, I was — what'd you say?

JAIME. Just … *(Pause.)*

29

— Yeah, I'm okay. Maybe I can do some writing.

CARRICK. You sure? *(Jaime nods, smiles.)* Okay … Next time. See you tomorrow. Have fun!

JAIME. Bye. *(Carrick goes into the house. Jaime puts her iPod back on, turns away from the house, starts to move to the music as she smokes. Carrick enters the kitchen. Sarah is finishing up with the cooler.)*

CARRICK. So I think I found out what's been bothering her.

SARAH. What?

CARRICK. Deena and Chris hooked up.

SARAH. Oh.

CARRICK. Remember that — your best friend / starts —

SARAH. So she's not coming?

CARRICK. Says she's gonna try to write.

SARAH. Oh well. You tried. And if she was gonna be in a pissy mood the whole time …

CARRICK. Maybe we shouldn't go. *(Pause.)*

SARAH. Why not?

CARRICK. I just — I think she's really down …

SARAH. Well — I mean, she's sixteen. She's gonna get — you know?

CARRICK. But she's been in this mood for — something seems, like — she says she's having trouble writing / she —

SARAH. Trust me, if we *don't* go, she'll feel *really* bad. She knows how hard we both worked all week to get the days / off.

CARRICK. *(Not really convinced.)* Right …

SARAH. *(Laughs.)* She gets like this a lot actually — the best thing you can do is ignore it.

CARRICK. Ignore it?

SARAH. She's a depressed — she's on Prozac. She's a depressed person, there's / nothing —

CARRICK. That doesn't mean you should ignore it, though.

SARAH. I'm not — I don't ignore it, that's not what I — but if you try to — what are you gonna do? Sit around all weekend and try to entertain her? Let her be in her mood, let her go through what she has to go through. She'll be fine, I promise.

CARRICK. I guess … *(Pause.)*

SARAH. It'll be nice, just the two of us.

CARRICK. That's true … *(Pause. Sarah moves to the cooler and duffle bag, picks them up.)*

SARAH. It's really sweet of you to offer — Got everything?

CARRICK. — Yeah, I think so. *(Carrick grabs the camping sup-*

plies. Sarah exits. Carrick follows, then pauses and turns towards the back. He calls out to the yard:) Bye, Jaime! *(Jaime doesn't hear him.)*

Scene 5

The next day. Evening. The cooler rests on the kitchen table. Sarah sits on the couch, looking through the photo album. The house is silent. Jaime comes down the stairs haltingly. She steps down into the living room.

JAIME. Hey … *(Sarah looks up at Jaime. Jaime wavers, steadies herself against the wall. Sarah rises.)*
SARAH.   Oh baby … *(Moving to her.)* Are you feeling better? *(Jaime looks down at her shirt, covered in dried vomit.)*
JAIME. What … *(Jaime looks blankly at the computer — the keyboard is turned over.)*
SARAH. Carrick went to the store to try to find stuff for it.
JAIME. What happened?
SARAH. It looked like you spilled soda on it. You don't remember? *(Pause. Jaime wavers again, moves to the kitchen table, steadies herself against it. Sarah goes to her.)* What did you do last night?
JAIME. I … I just took some Vicodin …
SARAH. How many? *(Pause.)*
JAIME. I don't remember.
SARAH. Did you drink anything?
JAIME. — It was stupid, I don't know why I did it.
SARAH. Who gave you the Vicodin?
JAIME. I just had them.
SARAH. From where? What were you thinking? *(We hear Carrick's car pull in. Jaime releases from the table, begins to walk to the stairs. She gets dizzy and holds onto the wall. Carrick enters, with a shopping bag. Sarah looks at him.)*
CARRICK. Sorry that took so long — Hey, Jaime. *(Jaime turns her head away.)* Got some stuff at Staples — see if we can get this keyboard working again. *(Jaime doesn't respond. Carrick and Sarah share a look. Then he crosses to the computer, sits down. Quietly, to Jaime:)* Were you working on a story, Jaime? *(Jaime looks at Carrick.)* The

guy at the store told me like fifty people a day come in and say they spilled something on their computer. Don't pass out on me. I need you. I don't want to ruin anything you need to save. *(Carrick gets up from the chair. Sarah steps away from Jaime. Jaime goes to the chair and sits. Sarah goes upstairs and off. Carrick moves into the kitchen.)* I'm gonna have a glass of water, you want one? *(Jaime doesn't answer. Jaime holds her head in her hands. Carrick gets two glasses of water, brings them over.)* Here you go. *(Carrick goes back to the computer, sits. He takes out cleaning supplies from the Staples bag and begins to clean the keyboard. He watches Jaime, who still holds her head in her hands.)* You didn't miss much not coming — it was kinda anti-climactic, the trip … *(Jaime doesn't respond. Pause.)* Were you looking at the photo album last night? That picture of you there? In the park, with Jason Carlyle? Wow. *(Jaime looks — sees the open photo album before her. She picks it up.)* Do you remember that, or were you too little?

JAIME. No. *(Pause. Carrick turns back to the computer, continues to clean it.)* I only have one memory of him. *(Carrick stops cleaning the keyboard, turns back to Jaime. She looks down at the album.)* I was on the kitchen floor. My mom and people were sitting at the table. It was smoky. I remember this guy was wearing my mom's pink night-gown. And he had really hairy legs. *(Pause. Jaime looks up at Carrick.)* That's it. *(Carrick smiles at her. A moment. Sarah comes down.)*

SARAH. I changed your sheets. *(Jaime puts down the album. She stands, goes upstairs, off. Carrick puts the keyboard aside, looks at Sarah.)* Throw up everywhere. She got Dominos delivered, there's two boxes up in her room, under her bed. Is that — can you smell it? Jesus. *(Sarah smells herself. Then she looks at the computer.)* Is it working?

CARRICK. No. The guy at Staples told me it was shot. Have to buy a new one, he said.

SARAH. Great, not even a year old — So what did you buy then?

CARRICK. Just this cleaner stuff, it was cheap.

SARAH. But why?

CARRICK. I just thought — so it would look like we tried to do / something. *(Sounds of vomiting from upstairs. Pause. A second wave, worse. Sarah exhales, goes upstairs, off. Carrick goes out back. He lights a cigarette, looks up at the sky. Sarah comes down the stairs, sees Carrick isn't in the living room. She goes out back, sits down in the doorway.)*

SARAH. "Get out, I'm fine."

CARRICK. They laid off the whole store tonight. *(Carrick turns to Sarah.)*

SARAH. What?

CARRICK. I got the call right after I went to go to Staples. Regional caught on, or somebody told, I don't know yet. They're keeping me and the other assistant manager and that's it. They fired Jack, they fired all the kids — told them they thought the store needed a fresh start, said they'd try to place them at other Goodys.

SARAH. I'm sorry.

CARRICK. They're not gonna place them, fucking liars. You know, and I'm driving back, feeling like shit, all those kids, you know, they're good kids — and I'm going through the stations, trying to find a song, something I can sing to, just to — and it was like, everything, every song was crap, you know? And I thought, this is fucking perfect.

SARAH. What is?

CARRICK. I love music, I work in a music store because I love music, and — there's not one not *one song* for me to sing to — and it's like — and Jaime, like — seeing her like — you could take her to a million shrinks, you know? It's not, the problem isn't her, you know, her brain chemistry or whatever — look around! Why should she be happy, what's there to be happy about?

SARAH. I don't understand, you're saying — she should be depressed?

CARRICK. I don't know what I'm saying, I'm just — I'm sad. Yeah, maybe I am — it's like last night. We're in the most beautiful place in the *world,* and those kids — on whatever drug they're on, playing Top 40 crap on their portable stereo, running around screaming — is everywhere just a club now? Look around, you're — this is what you do? How do you not join the party, the party's everywhere, everywhere you go! This is the world now, if that's not who you are, how do you *not* be depressed?

SARAH. You can not be depressed by doing what we did. You can move your tent.

CARRICK. That's not what I — what I'm saying is, you can't just ignore / this whole —

SARAH. You move the tent — I mean, you can bitch about the music and the kids, or enjoy the quiet place you moved your tent to.

CARRICK. It didn't piss you off, it didn't — *(Laughs.)* I couldn't get that fucking, that one song out of my head all night!

SARAH. Well, that's your responsibility. *(Pause.)*

CARRICK. Wait — what?

33

SARAH. That's — your / responsibility —

CARRICK. It's my responsibility to — I couldn't make them not play their music, I couldn't not hear a song / that was —

SARAH. I'm just saying, you can't let the world control how you feel. I used to do it, I used to hand my power over to "the world" and whenever I had a problem, you know, it was really convenient — bitch and moan about "the world," call my "friends" who felt the same way, *not* take responsibility, / *not* do anything to change —

CARRICK. I'm not — Sarah, it's not about blaming the world, just — I'm not trying to — I mean your daughter is, your daughter's passed out in a pool of her own vomit and you're saying, What did I do wrong, What did I do wrong. But it's not — you did a great job, Jaime's totally amazing — it's the way the world is, she's sensitive, she's an artist, the world's not — it's not made for her.

SARAH. So who's it made for then?

CARRICK. Whoever's — on drugs and listening to crap and not thinking about / anything —

SARAH. So you're saying give up.

CARRICK. No —

SARAH. You're saying, it's okay that she did / this, it's —

CARRICK. Sarah —

SARAH. — or, am I, am I not understanding you? It's a shitty world, that's what you're saying.

CARRICK. Yeah —

SARAH. And what I'm saying is, you have to create your own world.

CARRICK. Create your own — how do you do that?

SARAH. You move your tent, you get sober, you stop hanging out with bad friends — you do whatever, whatever you have to do, because if it's just a shitty world and there's nothing you can do, then I can just go drink and anyone can go do whatever they want because it's a shitty world, and no one has to look at their own actions / and no one —

CARRICK. Fine, if you don't want to listen — fine. *(Carrick laughs and turns away. Sarah stands.)*

SARAH. You know what actually? *(Beat.)* You're right — I don't want to listen. I listened to the shrink who put her on Prozac, I listened to the social worker who said take her out of school, I — Elaine who's telling her to write these stupid stories and talking about I have / no idea what —

CARRICK. *(Turning.)* Those stories are amazing, Sarah.

SARAH. Great, they're amazing, so what? There's a lot of people who are amazing at a lot of things, but unfortunately you have to live in the real world. You know, even if Elaine just told her, fine, write these stories, but also write *other* ones. That people will *like*. Even if Elaine just told her *that,* that would be teaching her to take responsibility. That's — you know what, I'm not paying for that anymore, that group. You know how much money / that woman —

CARRICK. The group means a lot to her.

SARAH. Because, because it's not the real world, because Elaine tells them what they want to hear. Jaime's not — nobody wants to read stories about fathers with their dicks hanging out / of their —

CARRICK. Sarah, just because the world doesn't — I mean, what if Jason thought, Oh, the world wants to be happy, I'll write happy / songs.

SARAH. Jason?

CARRICK. That music, if there hadn't been that music, it meant so / much to people —

SARAH. You're bringing up Jason as, what, / as —

CARRICK. I'm just saying — he wrote sad songs, and he made it. He didn't / write —

SARAH. He *made* it? He's *dead.*

CARRICK. Yeah, because of — fucking corporate media and commercial / rock —

SARAH. Oh, give me a break!

CARRICK. What? He talked about it in interviews! He talked about it all / the time —

SARAH. He didn't care about "corporate" whatever, "commercial" — he cared about one thing, he cared about getting *high.*

CARRICK. That's all he cared about? Have you ever listened to his *music?*

SARAH. He cared about getting *rich* so he could score, and getting *famous* so no one would stop him.

CARRICK. Have you listened *to his music?*

SARAH. — Are you gonna ask me that again.

CARRICK. Well, I'm just — then how can you talk that way about him?

SARAH. *Because I knew him.*

CARRICK. So, just because he / wasn't —

SARAH. He was an *addict* and a *liar.*

CARRICK. Sarah, he was the most / amazing

SARAH. He was a —

CARRICK. — artist —

SARAH. — *fraud. (More sounds of vomiting from upstairs. Sarah goes into the house, upstairs and off. Carrick takes a final drag on his cigarette, puts it out, and goes into the house. As he passes the photograph of Jaime, he stops. Pause. He takes the photograph down and opens the back. He removes the CD and slips it into his back pocket. He replaces the photograph on the wall, straightens it. Sarah begins down the stairs. Carrick picks up the water glasses and brings them to the sink. He begins to wash them. Sarah watches him a moment, then sits down at the kitchen table. Carrick looks, sees her. He shuts off the faucet, turns.)*

CARRICK. So … *(Sarah looks at him.)* Um — some people from work are getting together for a beer, so … impromptu farewell party …

SARAH. You're leaving? *(Pause.)*

CARRICK. I should, yeah … *(Sarah looks away. Carrick goes to her, kisses her on the head. Pause.)* — Bye. *(Carrick goes, off. Pause. We hear his car pull away. Sarah rises. She goes to the couch, picks up the photo album, looks at it. Jaime comes down the stairs.)*

JAIME. Was that Carrick? *(Sarah doesn't respond. Pause. Jaime crosses to the computer and sits. Sarah looks up. She shuts the album.)*

SARAH. He said it's broken. *(Sarah goes upstairs and off.)*

Scene 6

A few weeks later. Evening. Jaime is asleep on the couch, the television on. She is wearing pants that appear to be part of a uniform. The computer is without keyboard, plastic cover on it. Front door opens. Sarah enters, Phil follows.

PHIL. — It was a really hard thing for me, deciding if I had done the right thing or not. Because I felt like, Hey, she lied — Nice place! *(Sarah sees Jaime.)*

SARAH. What did I tell you.

PHIL. Supermarket work ain't easy!

SARAH. Jaime. Jaime. *(Sarah goes to Jaime. Phil sits down at the kitchen table. Sarah nudges Jaime awake.)* Jaime.

36

JAIME. *(Stirring.)* Wha…? *(Jaime sees Phil, sits up.)*

SARAH. How was work.

JAIME. *(Getting up.)* Fine. *(Jaime goes upstairs, off. Sarah goes to the kitchen.)*

PHIL. *(Smiles.)* About as talkative as my son.

SARAH. She's still getting used to working, she just started a couple weeks ago. So — wait, what did she lie about exactly?

PHIL. This is the way it works. Group uses twelve-step principles, but Martha isn't in recovery herself — she's a therapist, a social worker. So Martha also brings in other ideas, which is where the discussion topic comes in. The week before, I asked her what the topic of discussion was going to be for family night, and she said, "Dealing with change." And I thought, Fine, dealing with change, my mother can handle that.

SARAH. So everybody was bringing — *(Phil takes out cigarettes.)*

PHIL. — family members. Martha thought that it would open up communication about this aspect of our lives. A lot of times when you're in recovery, you can get into a bubble — do you mind if I smoke?

SARAH. — No, go ahead. *(Phil lights a cigarette. Sarah gets up, looks for an ashtray.)*

PHIL. So, I pick up my mother for family night, and she's drunk — which I expected, her being an alcoholic. *(A blast of music from upstairs.)* Whoa! *(Sarah sighs, brings over a saucer, sits.)* Hey, at least it isn't Britney. *(laughs.)* I tried to play my kid Bob Dylan the other day — he couldn't stop laughing. I said, Hey, this isn't funny, this music changed the world — he laughed even harder.

SARAH. *(Waving it off.)* I've learned to block it out.

PHIL. You must be pretty Zen! *(Laughs.)* So, we're driving to the meeting, I'm telling my mom about the people in group, I tell her about their jobs and their family situations, and she says, "I didn't know heroin addicts could live such normal lives." I thought, who knows, maybe this will really open her eyes — at least start a dialogue.

SARAH. Wait — so you're / not —

PHIL. You're wondering, Why do I go to AA if I'm a heroin addict.

SARAH. *(Laughs.)* Yeah.

PHIL. Every time I went to NA, I'd see a dealer, get offered drugs, see people smoking pot in the parking lot … Then you go into the meeting, and a lot of the testimony — to my mind, there was a lot of bragging going on, one-upmanship — I call it "romanticization." AA just seems a lot more sober to me — no pun intended.

37

SARAH. Gotcha.

PHIL. So, we get to group, and Martha says, "Hi everybody, welcome to family night. We start every meeting with a discussion topic, and tonight's topic is" — and I'm thinking, "dealing with change" — and Martha says, "the legacy of alcoholic parents." *(Pause.)* Exactly. Dead silence. Half the people in the room have alcoholic parents, and they're sitting there next to them! And Martha knows this — it's all we talk about! God, was I furious — my heart was pounding, I started to sweat ... finally the meeting ends, I bring my mother to the car, she hasn't said a word, I walk back, find Martha, and I say, "Excuse me, Martha. I have to tell you, I think that was really inappropriate. You know my mother is an alcoholic and you told me the discussion topic was going to be dealing with change."

SARAH. These therapists, it's unbelievable.

PHIL. She says, "I apologize if it made you uncomfortable. I thought it was a more suitable topic than dealing with change."

SARAH. That's it?

PHIL. That's it — totally avoided taking responsibility. But I have to say — you know, I thought about dropping out, and I came close — but finally I thought, you know — you have to show up for your life. You don't just walk away from a situation because you disagree, or because it's uncomfortable. You stick it out.

SARAH. Right ... *(Pause. Sarah looks at Phil, smiles.)*

PHIL. But enough about me — let me tell you about my mother! *(Phil laughs. Sarah laughs, rises.)*

SARAH. You want something to drink? Soda, water ...

PHIL. I'm all right — had quite a bit of coffee at the meeting. *(Sarah gets herself a water.)* How old was Jaime when you got sober?

SARAH. About seven.

PHIL. I caught my kid with a joint a couple of weeks ago, and he played the "You did it" card. Have you dealt with that one yet? *(Sarah comes back to the table with water, sits.)*

SARAH. Not that. But we've been dealing with other things, like taking responsibility, looking at your actions ...

PHIL. All good ones. I had no idea how to answer my son. It ended up leading to a much larger conversation. He had a lot of memories of when I was using, which we had never explored together. It was a pretty healing conversation — at least for me! Have you ever talked to Jaime about your drinking?

SARAH. You mean, like —

PHIL. — what it was like when you were drunk, for you, for her, the atmosphere …

SARAH. She was so young, I don't think she remembers. Plus I never really drank around her.

PHIL. Well — she probably remembers, just not "remembers" remembers.

SARAH. You mean like — repressed?

PHIL. No, that's psychobabble language. Like … all right, I'll just share this with you. My son's fifteen now. He was six when I got clean. Now, I never used around him, ever — but what he *did* remember was the emotional *atmosphere* of the time. I think kids really pick up on that, the *atmosphere* of using. *(Pause.)*

SARAH. I don't know exactly — what / you're —

PHIL. I'm not trying to say that / you —

SARAH. No, it's fine, I just —

PHIL. — were a bad mother or — believe me *(Laughs.)*. Here, this is what I mean. My dealer was this old Mexican grandfather. Lived in a two-bedroom apartment with his family — three generations, all addicts. I'd go over there, buy from him, talk to him for a little while about his family, and so on. When I stopped using, he would call me up and beg me to start buying from him again. He was broke and nobody in his family worked, and at the height of things, I had been giving him fifty, sixty dollars a day — so I had basically been supporting his whole family. He started calling me ten times a day, and a lot of times, my kid would answer the phone. He'd mumble in Spanish, crying — finally I told him if he called me again, I'd call the police. The next day, he shows up at my *house.* Crying, "Please, please." Said he'd give me the heroin for free.

SARAH. For free?

PHIL. Because he knew if I used just *once,* I'd be hooked again, instantly, and I'd start buying from him. He came by every day for a couple weeks. The *last* time I ever saw him, believe it or not, he asked me to buy the heroin *from* him and then give it back *to* him. He said he wanted to give it to his wife, who had this horrible back pain. He couldn't afford to buy his own heroin that he was selling.

SARAH. God.

PHIL. And my *son,* my son remembers this whole period of time. Only what *he* remembers is that I was mean to this sweet old man. *He* knew you were supposed to be nice to old men, so when he saw me hang up the phone or slam the door in the old man's face — that really shaped how he thought of me. *That's* what I mean by

39

atmosphere — all the things that are happening when you're using, not just the using itself.

SARAH. Right ... *(Pause.)* Did you see there's a sex addicts meeting now before AA?

PHIL. Someone told me that.

SARAH. Did you see the guys coming out?

PHIL. No.

SARAH. Sex addicts with who — that's what I want to know.

PHIL. *(Laughs.)* Senorita Internet. Senorita "World Wide Web." — I dated this woman once who would start crying if I didn't want to sleep with her.

SARAH. She'd cry?

PHIL. Yeah. If I was tired, or stressed out that day, and I didn't want to sleep with her — she'd just start to cry.

SARAH. What would you do?

PHIL. I'd hold her ... *(Pause. Sarah looks at Phil, makes eye contact with him. Leans in towards him, smiles. Pause.)* I haven't dated anyone in a while.

SARAH. No?

PHIL. I wanted to do some work on myself.

SARAH. I know about that ...

PHIL. Yeah. I'm getting there, though.

SARAH. Yeah?

PHIL. I'm starting to feel ready — What about you? Dated anybody recently? *(Pause. Sarah shakes her head "no." She leans in closer to Phil. Phil smiles, looks away. Then he looks back. Sarah kisses him. They kiss for a moment. Then Phil turns his head away again.)* So ... where do you work? *(Sarah smiles. Pause. She takes her glass of water, goes to the sink. Phil rises.)* I'm in a — bowling group, if you ever want to ... *(Sarah turns to Phil. Pause.)* You seem like a really interesting person. I'd like to get to know you better.

SARAH. Uh-huh?

PHIL. We get together every Monday night. I started the group myself. There's such a — we just don't connect in our culture. I call it a "longing to connect."

SARAH. Right ... I usually work on Mondays, so ...

PHIL. Well, if not bowling then — maybe I'll see you next Wednesday.

SARAH. Actually, I usually go to the meeting at First Church, so.

PHIL. Oh — the one with all the old guys? *(Sarah smiles. Pause.)* Well — thanks for inviting me over. *(Pause. Phil exits, off. Sarah looks towards the living room. She pauses, then moves to the photograph of Jaime hanging on the wall. She looks at it a brief moment, then takes it down and opens up the back. We hear Phil's car pull away. Sarah looks for the CD. She takes the back fully off, looks; slips out the photo, looks a second time — it isn't there. The music upstairs cuts off. Sarah looks towards the stairs, then quickly puts the picture back together. Jaime comes down the stairs just as Sarah hastily hangs the picture back up.)*

JAIME. Hey I'm going out, Deena's picking me up. *(Sarah turns away from the picture, which hangs, crooked.)*

SARAH. You're not going over there if her dad's around.

JAIME. We're just gonna drive around. *(Jaime goes into the kitchen. She sees the cigarette butt on the saucer, turns to Sarah.)* There's smoking in the house now? *(Sarah goes to the table, takes the saucer and brings it to the sink. Jaime opens the freezer, looks. Sarah cleans the saucer. Jaime takes out the pint of ice cream, gets a spoon, sits down at the table. She opens the ice cream and begins to eat. Sarah turns, sees.)*

SARAH. Jaime — use a bowl.

JAIME. There's only a little left. *(Sarah shuts off the faucet, turns to Jaime.)*

SARAH. How was work?

JAIME. Fine. *(Jaime eats a bite of ice cream.)*

SARAH. What else is going on.

JAIME. Nothing.

SARAH. *(Moving to kitchen table, sitting.)* What's your schedule, you working tomorrow?

JAIME. *(Taking another bite.)* In the morning.

SARAH. The morning? And you're going out now?

JAIME. I took a nap. *(Pause.)*

SARAH. What are you guys gonna do?

JAIME. Just drive around.

SARAH. Is Chris gonna be there?

JAIME. Yeah ... *(Pause.)*

SARAH. Don't you ever feel like a third wheel? *(Pause.)*

JAIME. No.

SARAH. Really? I would. *(Pause. Jaime takes a bite of ice cream.)* I wish there was somebody *you* liked. *(Jaime shrugs.)* Somebody from work or something ... you know?

JAIME. I don't mind. *(Jaime takes another bite of ice cream.)*

SARAH. Jaime — I don't know if you — how to say this ... *(Jaime looks at her mother.)* You really eat more than you should. *(Pause.*

Jaime puts the spoon down and walks out back. Sarah pauses a moment, then stands up, takes the ice cream, throws it away, puts the spoon in the sink. Outside, Jaime begins to cry. Sarah comes out back.) Jaime …

JAIME. What.

SARAH. I didn't mean that. I'm sorry.

JAIME. Okay. *(Pause.)*

SARAH. It's just — it's not an easy thing to talk about — your appearance. But if you want people / to —

JAIME. My appearance is fine.

SARAH. I'm just trying / to —

JAIME. It's fine.

SARAH. I noticed Deena started wearing different / clothes —

JAIME. Just leave me alone.

SARAH. I know the psychiatrist said one of the side-effects of the Prozac was, you know — you'd gain weight, but … do you ever look at yourself in the mirror? *(Jaime sucks on her cigarette, throws it down.)* Like in the bathroom mirror, after you get out of the shower / or —

JAIME. *(Turning.)* You fucking whore.

SARAH. What? *(Jaime moves towards the house. As she passes, Sarah grabs her.)* What did you call me?

JAIME. *(Crying.)* Fuck you you fucking whore! *(Jaime pulls herself away from Sarah, runs into the house. Sarah runs after her and grabs her, pulls her down to the floor.)*

SARAH. What did you call / me?

JAIME. Stop!

SARAH. What did you / call me?

JAIME. Get off!

SARAH. What did you say, what did you call / me —

JAIME. A fucking whore!

SARAH. A fucking whore, a fucking *whore* — *(Jaime swings her arm, elbowing Sarah in the mouth. Sarah cries out, covers her mouth.)*

JAIME. Oh God. Are you okay, are you okay? I'm sorry, I didn't — *(Sarah stands up, grabs Jaime's hair, pulls hard.)* Ow, ow ow ow *(Sarah pulls Jaime by the hair to the couch, throws her down. (Jaime tries to calm herself, breathes. Sarah goes to the freezer, gets ice, wraps it in a towel. She sits down at the kitchen table and presses the ice to her face. Her head is bowed down. Jaime notices the photograph on the wall, hanging crooked. She looks at it. Sarah lifts her head up, sees Jaime staring at the photograph. She watches her a moment. Then:)*

SARAH. What are you looking at? *(Jaime turns to Sarah.)*

JAIME. What.

SARAH. What are you looking at.

JAIME. Nothing.

SARAH. You were looking at the —

JAIME. — It's crooked.

SARAH. So what.

JAIME. Nothing.

SARAH. You were staring at it.

JAIME. No I wasn't. *(Pause.)*

SARAH. Did you take it? *(Pause.)*

JAIME. Take what.

SARAH. Don't lie to me, I can tell by the look / on your face —

JAIME. Take what?

SARAH. — where is it? *(Pause.)*

JAIME. — It's gone? *(Pause.)*

SARAH. How do you know. Did Carrick tell you.

JAIME. No.

SARAH. Did Carrick say / something —

JAIME. No!

SARAH. Where is it?

JAIME. I don't know.

SARAH. Maybe you took it out that night.

JAIME. What night?

SARAH. When we were on the mountain.

JAIME. I didn't.

SARAH. *(Standing.)* Maybe you don't remember! You don't remember spilling the soda all over the computer! You don't / remember —

JAIME. I didn't —

SARAH. — throwing up all over / yourself!

JAIME. I didn't!

SARAH. *(Coming at Jaime.)* HOW WOULD YOU REMEMBER.

JAIME. I remember, I / didn't —

SARAH. *(Closing in.)* HOW DO YOU KNOW / ABOUT IT.

JAIME. *(Cowering.)* I didn't — mom —

SARAH. *(Looming over her.)* HOW DO YOU KNOW. *(A horn honks from outside. Sarah turns towards the sound. Pause. Jaime runs out the front door, off. Sarah breaks into sobs. Sound of Deena's car driving away. Sarah curls onto the couch and cries. Jaime appears at the front door and enters. Sarah doesn't hear her. Jaime takes a few steps into the living room.)*

JAIME. Mom? *(Sarah opens her eyes, sees Jaime.)*
SARAH. DON'T LOOK AT ME LIKE THIS. DON'T LOOK
AT ME. *(Sarah cries, hides her face, curls into the couch. Jaime takes
another step towards her.)*
JAIME. Mom?
SARAH. WHY DOES EVERYONE LEAVE ME. WHY WHY?
(Jaime takes her iPod out of her pocket and approaches Sarah.)
JAIME. I have the song. *(Pause. Sarah opens her eyes and looks at
Jaime.)* Here. *(She hands her mother the iPod headphones. Sarah puts
them on. Jaime presses a button on the iPod.)* Do you hear it? *(Sarah
listens to the song. Then she rises, moves towards the kitchen, listening.
The cord pulls. She turns to Jaime, reaches out for the iPod. Jaime hands
it to her. Sarah moves into the kitchen, listening. Jaime looks to the wall,
where the crooked photograph of her hangs. She walks to it. She looks at
it a moment, then looks to her mother, in the kitchen, listening to the
song. Jaime turns back to the photograph. She looks at it a beat longer.
Jaime straightens the photograph. Then she turns and begins to walk out
back. Sarah looks to Jaime, sees her near the door.)*
SARAH. You going out with Deena? *(Jaime turns to her mother,
shakes her head "no.")* Where are you going? *(Pause.)*
JAIME. Just to have a cigarette. *(Jaime starts to go.)*
SARAH. Jaime — *(Jaime turns.)* I didn't mean to — it's just — it's
been a really hard time for me lately ... *(Pause. Jaime nods, then goes
out back. Sarah makes her way into the living room. Her whole body
now moves to the music, as if in reverie. As she passes the photograph,
she stops. She looks at it a moment, runs her finger across it ... Outside,
Jaime stands and looks up at the sky.)*

End of Play

PROPERTY LIST

Soda, iPod, (JAIME)
Cell phone (CARRICK)
Bouquet of roses (CARRICK)
Pocketbook (SARAH)
Short typed manuscript (JAIME)
Paper note (SARAH, CARRICK)
Bag of groceries (SARAH)
2 small bowls, ice cream, pint, spoons (SARAH, JAIME)
Photo album (SARAH)
Pen (CARRICK)
Sponge (SARAH)
CD (SARAH, JAIME, CARRICK)
Pizza (JAIME)
Sandwiches, sodas, cooler, duffle bag (SARAH, CARRICK)
Staples bag with computer cleaning supplies (CARRICK)
3 glasses of water (SARAH, CARRICK)
Cigarettes, lighter (CARRICK, JAIME, PHIL)
Saucer (SARAH)
Ice, towel (SARAH)

SOUND EFFECTS

Cell phone ring
Blast of music
Car arriving
Sounds of lovemaking
Sounds of vomiting
Car leaving
Horn honks

NEW PLAYS

★ **MATCH by Stephen Belber.** Mike and Lisa Davis interview a dancer and choreographer about his life, but it is soon evident that their agenda will either ruin or inspire them—and definitely change their lives forever. "Prolific laughs and ear-to-ear smiles." –*NY Magazine.* "Uproariously funny, deeply moving, enthralling theater. Stephen Belber's MATCH has great beauty and tenderness, and abounds in wit." –*NY Daily News.* "Three and a half out of four stars." –*USA Today.* "A theatrical steeplechase that leads straight from outrageous bitchery to unadorned, heartfelt emotion." –*Wall Street Journal.* [2M, 1W] ISBN: 0-8222-2020-2

★ **HANK WILLIAMS: LOST HIGHWAY by Randal Myler and Mark Harelik.** The story of the beloved and volatile country-music legend Hank Williams, featuring twenty-five of his most unforgettable songs. "[LOST HIGHWAY has] the exhilarating feeling of Williams on stage in a particular place on a particular night…serves up classic country with the edges raw and the energy hot…By the end of the play, you've traveled on a profound emotional journey: LOST HIGHWAY transports its audience and communicates the inspiring message of the beauty and richness of Williams' songs…forceful, clear-eyed, moving, impressive." –*Rolling Stone.* "…honors a very particular musical talent with care and energy… smart, sweet, poignant." –*NY Times.* [7M, 3W] ISBN: 0-8222-1985-9

★ **THE STORY by Tracey Scott Wilson.** An ambitious black newspaper reporter goes against her editor to investigate a murder and finds the *best* story…but at what cost? "A singular new voice…deeply emotional, deeply intellectual, and deeply musical…" –*The New Yorker.* "…a conscientious and absorbing new drama…" –*NY Times.* "…a riveting, tough-minded drama about race, reporting and the truth…" –*A.P.* "… a stylish, attention-holding script that ends on a chilling note that will leave viewers with much to talk about." –*Curtain Up.* [2M, 7W (doubling, flexible casting)] ISBN: 0-8222-1998-0

★ **OUR LADY OF 121st STREET by Stephen Adly Guirgis.** The body of Sister Rose, beloved Harlem nun, has been stolen, reuniting a group of life-challenged childhood friends who square off as they wait for her return. "A scorching and dark new comedy… Mr. Guirgis has one of the finest imaginations for dialogue to come along in years." –*NY Times.* "Stephen Guirgis may be the best playwright in America under forty." –*NY Magazine.* [8M, 4W] ISBN: 0-8222-1965-4

★ **HOLLYWOOD ARMS by Carrie Hamilton and Carol Burnett.** The coming-of-age story of a dreamer who manages to escape her bleak life and follow her romantic ambitions to stardom. Based on Carol Burnett's bestselling autobiography, *One More Time.* "…pure theatre and pure entertainment…" –*Talkin' Broadway.* "…a warm, fuzzy evening of theatre." –*BrodwayBeat.com.* "…chuckles and smiles of recognition or surprise flow naturally…a remarkable slice of life." –*TheatreScene.net.* [5M, 5W, 1 girl] ISBN: 0-8222-1959-X

★ **INVENTING VAN GOGH by Steven Dietz.** A haunting and hallucinatory drama about the making of art, the obsession to create and the fine line that separates truth from myth. "Like a van Gogh painting, Dietz's story is a gorgeous example of excess—one that remakes reality with broad, well-chosen brush strokes. At evening's end, we're left with the author's resounding opinions on art and artifice, and provoked by his constant query into which is greater: van Gogh's art or his violent myth." –*Phoenix New Times.* "Dietz's writing is never simple. It is always brilliant. Shaded, compressed, direct, lucid—he frames his subject with a remarkable understanding of painting as a physical experience." –*Tucson Citizen.* [4M, 1W] ISBN: 0-8222-1954-9

DRAMATISTS PLAY SERVICE, INC.
440 Park Avenue South, New York, NY 10016 212-683-8960 Fax 212-213-1539
postmaster@dramatists.com www.dramatists.com

NEW PLAYS

★ **INTIMATE APPAREL by Lynn Nottage.** The moving and lyrical story of a turn-of-the-century black seamstress whose gifted hands and sewing machine are the tools she uses to fashion her dreams from the whole cloth of her life's experiences. "…Nottage's play has a delicacy and eloquence that seem absolutely right for the time she is depicting…" –*NY Daily News*. "…thoughtful, affecting…The play offers poignant commentary on an era when the cut and color of one's dress—and of course, skin—determined whom one could and could not marry, sleep with, even talk to in public." –*Variety*. [2M, 4W] ISBN: 0-8222-2009-1

★ **BROOKLYN BOY by Donald Margulies.** A witty and insightful look at what happens to a writer when his novel hits the bestseller list. "The characters are beautifully drawn, the dialogue sparkles…" –*nytheatre.com*. "Few playwrights have the mastery to smartly investigate so much through a laugh-out-loud comedy that combines the vintage subject matter of successful writer-returning-to-ethnic-roots with the familiar mid-life crisis." –*Show Business Weekly*. [4M, 3W] ISBN: 0-8222-2074-1

★ **CROWNS by Regina Taylor.** Hats become a springboard for an exploration of black history and identity in this celebratory musical play. "Taylor pulls off a Hat Trick: She scores thrice, turning CROWNS into an artful amalgamation of oral history, fashion show, and musical theater…" –*TheatreMania.com*. "…wholly theatrical…Ms. Taylor has created a show that seems to arise out of spontaneous combustion, as if a bevy of department-store customers simultaneously decided to stage a revival meeting in the changing room." –*NY Times*. [1M, 6W (2 musicians)] ISBN: 0-8222-1963-8

★ **EXITS AND ENTRANCES by Athol Fugard.** The story of a relationship between a young playwright on the threshold of his career and an aging actor who has reached the end of his. "[Fugard] can say more with a single line than most playwrights convey in an entire script…Paraphrasing the title, it's safe to say this drama, making its memorable entrance into our consciousness, is unlikely to exit as long as a theater exists for exceptional work." –*Variety*. "A thought-provoking, elegant and engrossing new play…" –*Hollywood Reporter*. [2M] ISBN: 0-8222-2041-5

★ **BUG by Tracy Letts.** A thriller featuring a pair of star-crossed lovers in an Oklahoma City motel facing a bug invasion, paranoia, conspiracy theories and twisted psychological motives. "…obscenely exciting…top-flight craftsmanship. Buckle up and brace yourself…" –*NY Times*. "…[a] thoroughly outrageous and thoroughly entertaining play…the possibility of enemies, real and imagined, to squash has never been more theatrical." –*A.P.* [3M, 2W] ISBN: 0-8222-2016-4

★ **THOM PAIN (BASED ON NOTHING) by Will Eno.** An ordinary man muses on childhood, yearning, disappointment and loss, as he draws the audience into his last-ditch plea for empathy and enlightenment. "It's one of those treasured nights in the theater—treasured nights anywhere, for that matter—that can leave you both breathless with exhilaration and…in a puddle of tears." –*NY Times*. "Eno's words…are familiar, but proffered in a way that is constantly contradictory to our expectations. Beckett is certainly among his literary ancestors." –*nytheatre.com*. [1M] ISBN: 0-8222-2076-8

★ **THE LONG CHRISTMAS RIDE HOME by Paula Vogel.** Past, present and future collide on a snowy Christmas Eve for a troubled family of five. "…[a] lovely and hauntingly original family drama…a work that breathes so much life into the theater." –*Time Out*. "…[a] delicate visual feast…" –*NY Times*. "…brutal and lovely…the overall effect is magical." –*NY Newsday*. [3M, 3W] ISBN: 0-8222-2003-2

DRAMATISTS PLAY SERVICE, INC.
440 Park Avenue South, New York, NY 10016 212-683-8960 Fax 212-213-1539
postmaster@dramatists.com www.dramatists.com